Humanist

Celtic

Handfasting

(First Edition)

www.facebook.com/HumanistCelticHandfasting

Contents

Introduction

The Ceremony

Introduction

A Humanist Celtic style handfasting containing traditional elements modified to suit modern needs. There are no archaic word usages or references to deities or spirits.

This ceremony was used in our handfasting in the UK in 2015. Our family and friends of all ages, enjoyed taking an active part in the ceremony; none of them having had any previous experience of handfastings.

We developed this format because we felt the legal registry signing was too clinical and restrictive. We wanted something that reflected our feelings about marriage/civil partnership ceremonies and was inclusive of our family and friends who we also wanted to play a more active part than the official ceremonies allowed.

Looking solely at handfasting ceremonies we found that they invoked spirits and deities and were therefore not fully inclusive of all faiths and often attempted to reconstruct archaic language and structures which neither flowed or felt authentic. After extensive research, we developed the following ceremony which we hope you too will enjoy and will assist you in creating your own special day.

The language used in this ceremony should not offend people of any faith, or none, as it does not invoke any deity or belief system. Everyone at our handfasting enjoyed the experience and felt comfortable enough to take an active part in the ceremony. So, in that sense, it is a meaningful addition to signing the official register.

For the marriage/civil partnership ceremony to be legally binding in the UK it is required that the it includes the following:

Declaratory Words:

"I do solemnly declare that I know not of any lawful impediment why I (your name) may not be joined in matrimony to (partners name)"

And **Contracting Words**:

"I call up these persons here present to witness that I (your name) do take thee (partners name) to be my lawful wedded wife (or husband)" (this wording will vary for couples forming a Civil Partnership)

Are included as well as:

The couple formally identifying themselves to the registrar and signing the marriage/civil partnership register in front of two independent witnesses and a registrar.

You may wish to incorporate the above into your handfasting. However, as our chosen venue was unlicensed for marriage/civil partnership ceremonies we decided to attend the registry office with two witnesses where we signed the register and exchanged rings earlier the same day in order to become legally wed.

With a little adaptation, it is therefore possible to combine this ceremony with an official signing of the register. To do this you will need to contact the local registry office and ensure that your setting possesses the required license as well as your proposed arrangements conforming to UK law.

I understand that most offices are quite friendly and are normally prepared to discuss your requests and offer assistance to make your day proceed as you wish it to, within legal parameters. There are also local professionals who offer services to couples who are able to advise and arrange this. Quite often your chosen venue will either have arrangements with such people or will know of reliable individuals who can help you.

The ceremony is written as for a mixed gender couple, but it can also be used by same sex couples. There is no difference between the words used by either participant. Indeed, no part of the ceremony should be regarded as fixed. This should simply be thought of as a *pro forma* for the final ceremony you will use.

Pre Planning

You should plan such an event several months in advance to give everyone, including yourselves, plenty of time to put everything required in place.

You should also ensure that the proprietor of any premises or land on or in which you intend to hold your ceremony is aware and happy for you to proceed. If it's going to be combined with an official registration of marriage/civil partnership ceremony it will need to be licensed anyway, but even if you intend to do this as a separate ceremony, you should clearly explain your intentions to them, perhaps in writing. A few may object or may be concerned that what you are doing is legal. In any event no one wants a bad surprise on the day.

The Primary Participants

In addition to the guests and of course the bride and groom, the celebration requires handmaidens (similar to bridesmaids) one of whom is required to read a poem and a flower girl who can be under the care and direction of another handmaiden. There is also a role for a best man to read a blessing. (These of course could be read by any guest, or indeed the bride and/or groom.) A celebrant is also required.

The celebrant can be anyone who is reliable, has a good strong voice and enjoys public presentation. Their confidence and comfort with the process is key to its success. If you know an actor, performance poet or orator of some kind, they may well be a great choice. They should dress accordingly. We used a friend who engages in historical re-enactment as a hobby and also makes medieval dresses as a profession. She hugely enjoyed the occasion and most effectively wore a beautiful handmade cloak over her dress during the ceremony.

The Setting

You can choose or adapt your setting to suit any personal preferences or themes that are significant to you. If the setting is outdoors, you need to consider what to do if it's raining or excessively windy. In the interests of safety, you may consider not having a candle involved for an outdoor ceremony as turning the celebrant into a living torch may put something of a dampener on events and, in high wind, they can be difficult to keep alight. In any event the celebrant should be made very aware that the candle is behind them and they should not step back into it. If this is in an issue don't use the candle!

I recommend a circle is previously marked on the floor, if you chose to use one. I suggest using a thick coloured rope or cord about 9 metres long (or 9 yards) formed into a 3 metre (9 feet) diameter circle, you will find attractive cord in curtain shops (drapes stores). This is where the ceremony itself will take place and where the three primary participants; Bride, Groom and Celebrant will stand. 3 metres diameter is amply sufficient for this purpose and the circumference is large enough for up to around 40 guests to stand whilst keeping a pathway clear for the bride to walk down. (A video camera could be placed on a tripod at a point outside the circle after the bride's arrival to film the event should that be required.)

Behind the circle (and celebrant) is a small, tall table (we used a round one, a small occasional table should suffice) on which is placed a goblet large enough to comfortably hold between 5 and 7 ml of wine per participant, perhaps a special purchase for the event or a family heirloom. The goblet should be easy to handle and pass around while full, without spilling, (guests will be upset if their clothing is ruined with red wine spilled from a too small goblet.) The wine should be fortified as this is more hygienic. Sherry or Port is ideal or communion wine can be used (bought from church suppliers). I suggest red on aesthetic grounds and we used a good quality Ruby Port. A napkin should accompany the goblet so that guests may wipe the goblet before supping. A large candle should also be placed upon the table. This is lit to denote the very beginning of the celebration and extinguished to denote the end.

Most important is the cord used to 'hand fast' the couple. The cord needs to be quite long, longer than you might imagine. I would suggest the final cord should be approximately 2.5 metres long and be finished with a significant and tasteful metal or christal token to weight it to assist in the process of binding. We used plaited silk with three symbolic colours representing passion, fidelity, and new beginnings. You may have ideas of your own that will be significant to you but I would suggest at least 3 or 4 colours. The resultant cord, in our case shimmered in peacock colours and is a thing of beauty. We intend to keep this as a keepsake of the event. Traditionally they were placed over the marriage bed as a lifelong reminder of the partnership. Depending on how tight the plaiting is, to make a 2.5 metre cord you need perhaps 3 times its final length in each colour. The result should be substantial and around 1cm thick. Traditionally the couple would create the handfasting cord themselves some time prior to the ceremony but this could also be donated as a gift. When making your choice you may wish to research which option you would prefer.

If you are incorporating an exchange of rings as part of the handfasting then they too will of course be required but we chose to exchange our rings during the service at the Registry Office.

Care & Safety

When planning, as with any event, all care should be taken to ensure the setting is safe. Safety around candles is important, particularly if there are young children present who may have a short attention span and possibly become fractious. Don't forget not only is the flame potentially dangerous but also the molten wax created is highly hazardous. Make sure there are no trip hazards especially if you are in a wood; including the approach so that the bride does not need to pick her way down the 'aisle' avoiding tree roots or debris and while most of your guests will be required to stand for the short ceremony, you may want to provide seating for older guests who may find this a challenge. You may also wish to consider any necessary mobility or other issues to ensure that guests are comfortable, safe and enabled to participate.

The Ceremony

Flower Girl enters followed by Handmaidens and Bride. Groom stands at the side of the Celebrant within the circle. Celebrant lights the candles.

Bridal music plays, bride enters...

Flower girl scatters flower petals as she enters including if required over each table in turn and then around the outside of the circle. Bride joins Groom and Celebrant inside the circle whilst Chief Handmaiden stands to her side outside the circle. The Flower Girl and other Handmaiden stands to the Celebrant's side outside the circle.

Celebrant: Would everyone please join us and gather round the circle.

Introduction

Celebrant: Welcome everyone to *[Bride's Name]* and *[Groom's Name]*'s handfasting ceremony. Before we start can I ask that everyone please turn off their mobile phones and any other devices for the duration of the ceremony to avoid any interruptions? Thank you.

[Bride's Name] and *[Groom's Name]* would like me to pass on their deepest gratitude to you all for coming. It is very important to them that so many of their nearest and dearest can be here to support them in making this commitment to each other and celebrate with them the joy of this occasion. I know that making the journey took considerable effort for many of you and for this they are truly appreciative.

For the benefit of those who only know one of them well, I'd like to introduce *[Bride's Name]* and *[Groom's Name]* to you all.

[one party's guests may not know the other

party to the handfasting too well, so you might consider adding a short bio of both the bride and groom, it doesn't have to be detailed but just a little about them. It can be light hearted and may help to relax people a little; this can become more interesting the more life experience each has had. It should include a little about the history of the relationship, concluding with their intent to commit themselves to each other.]

This brings us to the reason why we are here today.

Handfasting Explanation

Celebrant: *[Bride's Name]* and *[Groom's Name]* have chosen to incorporate the ancient Celtic ritual of handfasting into their wedding ceremony. Handfasting may be unfamiliar to many of you so I will explain a little about it.

A handfasting was originally more like an engagement period or trial marriage, where two people would declare a binding union between themselves for a year and a day.

After a year went by, the couple could either separate as if they had never been married or decide to permanently enter into a full marriage.

In later times it was performed as a form of common law marriage. Handfasting was suppressed following the Synod of Whitby in 664 but was still considered amongst many as a legal form of marriage in England until 1753 when it was outlawed. In Scotland it continued until 1939 – remember the stories of elopement to Gretna Green to be married over the anvil?

Incorporated into the ceremony is a symbolic binding of the hands which inspired the terms 'bonds of holy matrimony' and 'tying the knot'… the handfasting. The coloured cords used for the binding in today's ceremony are red representing passion, blue for fidelity and green for new beginnings.

Throughout history, in many ways and in many parts of the world, the hands of the bride and groom were bound as a sign of their commitment to each other. Rings were only for the very rich; love knows no such bounds. These perishable bonds are a reminder that all material things eventually return to the earth, unlike the bond and connection of love, which is eternal.

Legal Marriage/civil partnership ceremony now of course must be performed by an authorised registrar - usually a member of the clergy or someone appointed by the council – and indeed *[Groom's Name]* and *[Bride's Name]* performed this part of their marriage/civil partnership ceremony this afternoon at the registry office here in *[location]*. The handfasting ceremony here today is the personal side of *[Bride's Name]* and *[Groom's Name]* showing their commitment to each other amongst their family and friends.

Preamble

[Bride's Name] and *[Groom's Name]*, We are indeed encircled by your family and friends, who are gathered to witness your exchange of vows and share in the joy of the occasion. Let this ceremony be a statement of what you mean to each other and the commitment you make. Sharing life's celebrations is important to us all.

Expression of intent

Celebrant: Within this circle, you are declaring your love and life commitment to each other. The promises made today and the ties that are bound here will strengthen your union across the years of your lives as you continue to grow closer together.

They are a reminder to you and to others in the days and years to come of the important principles of partnership, love and respect.

[Bride's name] *[Groom's name]* Do you seek to enter this handfasting ceremony of your own free will?

[Bride's Name] **and** *[Groom's Name]*: Yes.

Celebrant (*turning to the guests*): Today, you have come here not simply to witness our couple's union, but to take part in it. Each of you represents not only yourself, but all of the people who have and will touch the lives of *[Bride's Name]* and *[Groom's Name]*. Your support has helped their relationship to flourish, and the joy that you all bring into the couple's lives sustains them. Do you promise to stand beside them, support them without judgement, listen to them with an open heart and love them without condition?

Guests: We do

Sharing of the Chalice

(Celebrant holds the cup)

The years of life are as a cup of wine. It is both bitter and sweet. The sweetness of life is found in joy, hope, peace, love, happiness and delight. The bitterness of life is found in its trials and tribulations; disappointments sorrows grief and despair.

Together the sweet and the bitter represent life's journey and all the experiences that are naturally a part of it and by sharing this cup, we enhance life's sweet joys and ease its bitter sorrows.

As you all share the wine from the loving cup *(Celebrant raises the cup)* you undertake to share whatever the future brings. It represents the blessing given and passed on to each participant in this ceremony.

Drink now and may the cup of your lives be sweet and full to running over.

(Celebrant passes the cup to [Bride's Name], then [Groom's Name], partakes herself and then the chalice starts its journey around the circle clockwise)

*(recital of poem by **handmaiden** during the sharing of the chalice)*

> Love is giving, not taking
> Mending, not breaking,
> Trusting, believing
> Never deceiving
> Patiently bearing
> And faithfully sharing
> Each joy, every sorrow
> Today and tomorrow
> Love is kind, understanding
> But never demanding
> Love is constant, prevailing
> Its strength never failing.
> A promise once spoken
> For all time unbroken,
> A lifetime together
> Love's time is for ever.   *(Anon)*

(The cup continues to travel around the circle as the ceremony continues)

Handfasting Vows

Celebrant: *[Bride's Name]* and *[Groom's Name]*, please hold hands. (*Hold hands, one partner with his or her left hand and the other with his or her right hand or however you feel most comfortable.*)

Celebrant: *[Bride's Name]* and *[Groom's Name]*, will you honour and respect one another?

[Bride's Name] and [Groom's Name]: I will (*part of the cord is wrapped around their hands*)

Celebrant: Will you support and assist each other in times of pain?

[Bride's Name] and [Groom's Name]: I will (*another part of the cord is wrapped around their hands*)

Celebrant: Will you share each other's laughter, joy and dreams?

[Bride's Name] and [Groom's Name]: I will

(more of the cord is wrapped around their hands)

Celebrant: Will you work together in difficult and challenging times and look to the positives in each other?

[Bride's Name] **and** *[Groom's Name]*: I will *(more of the cord is wrapped around their hands)*

Celebrant: Will you have the courage and commitment to remember these promises with an open heart should you falter?

[Bride's Name] **and** *[Groom's Name]*: I will *(The rest of the cord is wrapped around their hands)*

Celebrant: *[Bride's Name]* and *[Groom's Name]*, as your hands are now bound together, so your lives and spirits are joined in a union of perfect love and perfect trust. The bond of marriage/civil partnership ceremony is not formed by these cords, but by the vows you have made. For always you hold in your own hands the fate of this union.

[Best man's name] will now read a blessing.

Blessing

*(read by **Best man**)*

> Above you are stars
>   and below you the earth.
> Like stars your love will be
>   a constant source of light,
> and like the earth, a firm foundation
>   from which to grow.
>
> May your hands always hold each other
>   during the storms of life.
> May they be tender and gentle
>   as you nurture each other.
> May they build a relationship founded
> in
>   love, rich in caring,
> May your hands heal, protect, shelter,
>   and guide each other.

Pronouncement and Kiss

[Bride's Name] and [Groom's Name], on behalf of all those present, and by the strength of your own love, I pronounce you hand-fasted.

May you know nothing but happiness from this day forward,
may the road rise to meet you,
may the wind be always at your back,
may the warm rays of sun fall upon your home,
may the hand of a friend be always near,
may the grass beneath your feet be green,
may the sky above you be blue,
may the joys that surround you be pure,
may the hearts that love you be true.

You may seal your vows with a kiss.

(the celebrant unties the couple.)

Conclusion

Groom *thanks those who helped the day [similar to a traditional speech]*

Celebrant: Friends and family, please feel free to congratulate the couple. *Celebrant also offers any other instructions regarding the rest of the evening and what will happen next.*

Printed in Great Britain
by Amazon

36598683R20020